A Trip to the Aquarium

by Becky Manfredini

HOUGHTON MIFFLIN HARCOURT

PHOTOGRAPHY CREDITS: (c) ©Renata Souza e Souza/Flickr Open/Getty Images; 3 (b) ©Image Source/Getty Images; 4 (b) ©Renata Souza e Souza/Flickr Open/Getty Images; 5 (b) ©Sandy Felsenthal/Documentary Value/Corbis; 6 (b) ©Nick Rains/Encyclopedia/Corbis; 7 (t) ©Thomas Sbampato/Imagebroker/Alamy Images; 8 (b) ©Blaine Harrington III/Terra/Corbis; 9 (t) ©Mauricio Handler/National Geographic/Corbis; 10 (b) ©John Gress/Corbis Wire/Corbis; 11 (b) ©RICHARD HANSEN/Photo Researchers/Getty Images

Printed in Mexico

ISBN: 978-0-544-07235-0

10 0908 20 19 18 17

4500669231   A B C D E F G

Contents

Vocabulary	Stretch Vocabulary
living things	aquarium
nonliving things	exhibit
environment	caregiver
shelter	kelp
	vet

Introduction

Welcome to the aquarium! An aquarium is a place used for showing living things in water environments.

You will see many exhibits during your visit. These are areas where you can watch sea life. Look around, or you will miss tiny fish. You may even see a big shark! You will also meet caregivers who take care of the water plants and animals.

You can touch things at this exhibit.

Living Things at the Aquarium

How are fish, water animals, and water plants the same? They are living things, or things that are alive. You will see many living things at the aquarium. Plants and animals need food, water, and air to live. They also need space to move and grow. They are living things with needs—just like you!

Living things change and grow.

Nonliving Things at the Aquarium

What are nonliving things that you might see at the aquarium? The water that some birds swim in is nonliving because it is not alive. The sand that the birds walk and rest on is nonliving, too. The birds live in an environment. An environment is made up of all the living and nonliving things in a place.

What are some things in a penguin's environment?

Sea Otters and Their Environment

Sea otters live in an ocean environment. Their exhibit is filled with lots of salty ocean water. Sea otters live in groups. When they want to sleep, they find seaweed called kelp for shelter. A shelter is a place where animals can be safe. The sea otters wrap themselves in kelp. Now they can stay together, not drift away, and be protected while they nap!

Sea otters use kelp for shelter.

Sea otters eat other sea animals.

It is time to feed the sea otters! The caregiver will feed them their favorite meal of crab and clams. First the sea otters float on their backs. Then they put a crab or clam on their chest. They use a rock to crack open the shell and eat the food inside. Yum!

Caregivers Dive In!

Another ocean environment in the aquarium is the kelp forest. Caregivers dive into the tank.

The caregivers will trim the kelp that grow fast. They will check the temperature of the water to make sure it is not too warm or too cool. They will clean the tank, too.

Kelp grows quickly.

Small fish eat kelp. Then bigger fish eat them!

Do you know what kelp is used for in the ocean? Smaller fish and water animals use it for shelter. They can hide from bigger fish that want to eat them! Kelp is also food for sea urchins. These are small water animals with spiny shells.

At the Animal Health Lab

Do you ever go to the doctor's office for a checkup? Then you are just like the water animals at the aquarium! They go to the animal health lab and visit the vet. A vet is an animal doctor. Vet is short for veterinarian.

The vet makes sure that the penguin is healthy.

Saving Water Animals

The caregivers who work at the aquarium study fish, water animals, and plant-like living things. Sometimes, the caregivers save injured animals. The workers care for the animals until they get better. Then the animals are released back into the ocean when they are healthy. Caregivers learn a lot about sea life. They are caregivers because they care!

The green tag lets caregivers track this sea otter.

Become a Caregiver!

Draw a picture of a kelp forest at the aquarium. Draw yourself in the picture. Show how you trim the kelp or feed the water animals and fish. Write a short paragraph about your picture. Read it to a friend.

 Make a Word and Picture List

Find an aquarium that is near your community. Use the Internet to help you. Write the names of the water animals and fish that live there. Draw a picture of each one.